A First Book of
Jewish Bible Stories

Stories retold by
Mary Hoffman
Illustrated by
Julie Downing

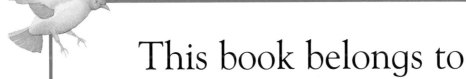

This book belongs to

....

A DK Publishing Book

For Anna-Louise
and William

LONDON, NEW YORK, MUNICH,
PARIS, MELBOURNE, DELHI

Project Editors Lee Simmons
and Nicola Deschamps
U.S. editorial Camela Decaire,
Lenny Hort, and Beth Sutinis
Designers Sheilagh Noble
Jacket design Karen Shooter
Additional design Jo Malivoire and Emy Manby
DTP Designer Louise Paddick
Production Shivani Pandey
Managing Editor Jane Yorke
Managing Art Editor Chris Scollen
Religious Consultants Donald Kraus, Jenny Nemko, and
Rev. Terence Handley McMath

First American Edition 2002
Published in the United States by DK Publishing, Inc.
95 Madison Avenue, New York, New York 10016

2 4 6 8 10 9 7 5 3 1

Copyright © 2002 Dorling Kindersley Limited

A revised excerpt from
A First Bible Story Book

Text Copyright © 1997, 2002 Mary Hoffman

Hoffman, Mary, 1945-
  A first book of Jewish Bible stories / by Mary Hoffman ;
illustrated by Julie Downing.
    p. cm.
  ISBN 0-7894-8504-4
  1. Bible stories, English--O.T. 2. Bible.
O.T.--Biography--Juvenile literature. [1. Bible stories--O.T.]
I.
Downing, Julie, ill. II. Title.
  BM107 .H64 2002
  221.9'505--dc21

2001047618

Reproduced by GRB Editrice, S.r.l. of Italy
Printed and bound in Italy by L.E.G.O.

see our complete catalog at
www.dk.com

Contents

God Makes the World

In the very beginning, there was nothing but emptiness, darkness, and deep, deep water. Then God said the word, and the world was filled with light. He had made the first day.

But He saw that darkness was good, too, so He kept it and called it night.

On the second day, God divided up the water. Some He made the sea. The rest He put up in the sky. He made heaven to keep them apart.

On the third day, God put the seas in their proper places, and dry land between them. He told the earth to start growing trees and grass and plants.

On the fourth day,
He made two big
lights to hang in
the sky – the
sun by day . . .

and the
moon by night.
Then He made
the stars that
keep them
company.

On the fifth day,
    God made all the creatures that
        live in the water – fish,
            whales, dolphins,
                and octopuses.

Then He made all
the birds that fly
in the air, from the
great eagle to the
tiny wren.

But the sixth day was the busiest of all. God made all the animals that live on the land. Not just the big ones, like buffaloes and elephants and tigers, but everything, right down to the smallest beetle

He decided to make some people,
too, who would be like Him.
He made a man and a woman
to take care of all the animals.
God saw that the world He
had made was good. On
the seventh day, He rested.

that creeps through the grass.

The first man and woman were
Adam and Eve. God gave them a
wonderful garden called Eden. He told
them to eat fruit and plants and take care
of every single living thing in the world. He
told them that every person in the world
would come from them and their children.

The first job God gave Adam and Eve was to name all the animals. Imagine trying to choose the right name for the camel, the giraffe,

or the ostrich if you didn't know it already!

God visited Adam and Eve in the garden and talked to them. He gave them only one rule. "See that tree over there in the middle of the garden?" He asked. "It is the Tree of Knowledge. You must never eat its fruit. If you do, you will die."

Now there was a snake in the garden.
It slithered up to Eve and hissed,
"Why don't you pick that ripe
fruit from the tree in the
middle of the garden?"

Eve said, "God told us
not to. If we do, we will
die." "Nonsense," said
the snake. "This fruit
will help you know
secrets that God doesn't
want you to know."

The fruit looked tasty, so Eve picked one and took a big, juicy bite. It was so good she shared some with Adam. Right away, they felt shy and ashamed and realized they had no clothes on.

As soon as God realized they had eaten the forbidden fruit, a sadness as big as the whole world came over Him.

He gave them clothes and sent them out of the garden to raise their children and live without ever seeing Eden again. To make sure they couldn't return, He set an angel with a fiery sword at the gate. And all because they had done the one thing He had asked them not to do.

Noah's Ark

Hundreds of years after Adam and Eve, the world had filled up with wicked people. This made God sad. He saw that there was only one good family left on the Earth: Noah, his wife, and their three sons, Shem, Ham, and Japheth.

God said to Noah, "I am going to send a great flood to wash the Earth clean. Everyone will be drowned except you and your family. You must build a big boat. You'll need space for a lot of food because there will be many animals to feed."

"Animals?" asked Noah. "Yes," said God. "Two of each kind, a male and female, including birds and creepy crawlies – even snakes."

God told Noah exactly how to build the boat, which was called an ark. Noah's whole family had to help – all his sons and their wives – because they would all be on the ark. They painted the wooden ark with sticky tar to keep the water out.

Noah's neighbors thought he was crazy. "A boat!" they laughed. "Haven't you noticed there's no sea around here?" But Noah kept on building.

As soon as the ark was ready, Noah took out his list of animals. His family had been rounding them up for weeks. How the neighbors stared! Two by two, the animals entered the ark.

The bears lumbered, the reindeer pranced, the giraffes swayed, and the snakes slithered.

The elephants were terribly slow, the lions padded along, the parrots squawked, and the wolves howled. The swift cheetahs passed right by the crawling crocodiles and leaping kangaroos.

Soon the ark was alive with animals.
It was full of hay and oats and food for the
family, too. But the sky was getting very dark.
"Hurry up!" cried Noah to the waddling penguins.
As the tortoises crept up the gangplank, the first
drops of rain began to fall.

It was as if God had opened a window in heaven and poured
water out. Rain cascaded from the sky, filling all the valleys.
Thunder rumbled and lightning flashes cracked the sky in two.

For 40 days and 40 nights, rain drummed on the roof of
the ark. Then one morning everything was quiet. The rain
had stopped and the sun was shining again.

The people who had laughed at Noah were now desperate to escape the rising water, but only the ark was lifted safely to the top of the swirling water, higher than the mountaintops.

The ark drifted for months. At last it bumped into some rocks. Slowly, the floodwaters sank down. Noah saw that the ark had settled on the high mountaintops of Ararat.

The animals couldn't wait to get off! But Noah wanted to be sure it was safe. Three times he sent a dove out from the ark.

The first time the dove flew straight back. The second time it had an olive leaf in its beak. The third time the dove didn't come back at all. It had found somewhere green and fresh to live. So Noah let down the gangplank and the animals bounded out of the ark.

As the birds flew away, Noah saw a beautiful arch of colors glowing in the sky. It was the first rainbow. God promised that He would never again destroy life on Earth. The rainbow would remind Him of His promise.

Abraham and His Family

After the Flood, Noah's family grew and grew, peopling the Earth. One of these people became very special to God. The man's name was Abraham. His wife was Sarah.

One day, God sent for Abraham and told him that if he went where God led him, he would become the father of a great new nation.

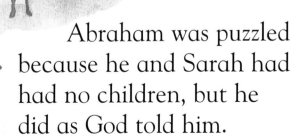

Abraham was puzzled because he and Sarah had had no children, but he did as God told him.

Abraham gathered all his people together and, with Sarah and his nephew Lot, set out for Canaan. When they were nearly there, Lot and his people decided to turn to the East . . .

and Abraham and Sarah went to the West.

God spoke to Abraham again, telling him that all the land around him would belong to him and his family. He also said that Sarah would have a son. "Your family will be as many as there are stars in the sky," He said. Abraham was amazed. Surely Sarah was too old to have a child?

21

Sarah was very surprised to have a baby at last. They named their son Isaac.

When Isaac was still a little boy, God decided to give Abraham a terrible test. He wanted to see how much Abraham loved Him. God told him to take Isaac up a high mountain and kill him. Abraham was horrified, and he could not tell Sarah what God had said.

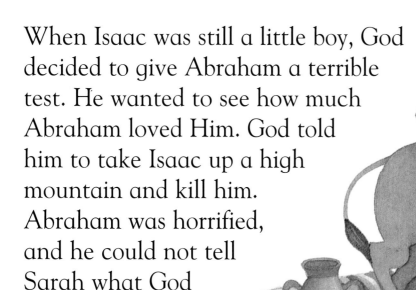

He loaded a donkey and took Isaac with him as if they were just going out for a picnic.

Isaac carried wood, and they set off to climb the mountain.

When they had reached the top, Abraham built an altar and piled the wood on top. Isaac thought his father was going to kill a lamb. "Father, where is the lamb?" asked Isaac. "God will provide a lamb," said Abraham, but he could hardly speak for tears.

He set Isaac on the altar and took out his knife. The boy was terrified. Suddenly an angel called out, "Stop! Now God knows how much you love Him – you were ready to give Him your only son." Looking up, Abraham saw a ram in the bushes, which he killed instead of Isaac.

Abraham had passed the test. He hugged Isaac tightly, then took him back home.

Joseph and His Rainbow Coat

When Isaac grew up he married Rebekah and they had twin sons, Esau and Jacob. Jacob, who was also called Israel, settled in Canaan and had a large family. His 12 sons were named . . .

Reuben, Simeon, then Levi and Judah, Issachar and Zebulun,

Gad and Asher, Dan and Naphtali, then Joseph and Benjamin.

Joseph and Benjamin were Jacob's favorite children, but he loved Joseph best of all.

One day Joseph told his brothers about a dream he had had. They were tying up grain in the fields when . . .

. . . all the other brothers' bundles bowed down to Joseph's.

Joseph's dream made his brothers really angry. "Who does he think he is?" they grumbled.

Jacob gave Joseph a beautiful coat, colored like a rainbow, and that made the brothers even more jealous. They hated Joseph so much that some of them wanted to harm him.

So one day while they were working in the fields, they grabbed Joseph and tore his splendid coat off him. They decided to kill Joseph and throw his body into a well.

But Reuben disagreed and said, "Let's just leave him at the bottom of the well." Reuben secretly meant to come back later and rescue Joseph.

Later, while Reuben was busy, the other brothers sold Joseph to some merchants who were traveling to Egypt.

Then the brothers smeared the rainbow coat with goat's blood and told Jacob his favorite son had been killed by a wild beast.

When the merchants reached Egypt, they sold Joseph to the captain of Pharaoh's guard. Joseph worked hard and after some years he was made head of the household.

One day, Pharaoh had a nightmare that no one could explain. God had shown Joseph what other people's strange dreams meant. So the Pharaoh sent for him.

In Pharaoh's dream, seven fat cows came out of the river to graze.

Then seven thin cows followed the fat cows out of the water and gobbled them up. But the thin cows didn't get any fatter.

Joseph told Pharaoh that the dream meant Egypt was going to have seven years of good harvests followed by seven years of famine.

Pharaoh was so impressed by Joseph's explanation that he put him in charge of building barns to store extra food for the bad years. And Pharaoh's dream came true, just as Joseph said.

Years later, during the famine, 11 visitors came from Canaan to ask for food. They were Joseph's brothers. He knew who they were immediately, but they had no idea who this powerful Egyptian was. Joseph decided to test his brothers to see if they had changed.

He gave them all the food they could carry, but in Benjamin's sack he hid a special silver cup.

The brothers set off for home, but they had not gone far when Joseph's guards rode after them and found the cup in Benjamin's sack.

The brothers were arrested and brought to Joseph. He pretended to be angry. "The rest of you can go free," he said, "but the one who stole my cup shall stay and be my slave."

The other brothers were horrified. Their father had already lost one of his favorite sons – it would break his heart if they went back without Benjamin. "Take one of us instead," they begged.

Then Joseph knew they had really changed. He told them who he was and asked them to fetch Jacob so they could all live together in Egypt.

Moses in the Bulrushes

Jacob's family, the Israelites, grew very large. Long after Joseph and his brothers were dead, there were lots of them living in Egypt. The new Pharaoh did not like so many Israelites being in his country.

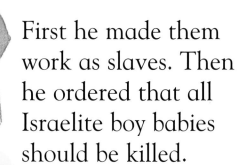

First he made them work as slaves. Then he ordered that all Israelite boy babies should be killed.

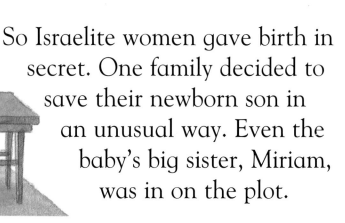

So Israelite women gave birth in secret. One family decided to save their newborn son in an unusual way. Even the baby's big sister, Miriam, was in on the plot.

They kept the baby hidden till he was three months old. By then he was sleeping less and it was hard to keep him a secret. So his mother wove a basket out of reeds. Miriam helped.

They coated the basket with mud and tar and let it dry. It was like a tiny boat.

The baby's mother put him in his little basket-boat and carried him to the river. She put the basket gently in the water, where it was half-hidden by bulrushes and reeds.

Pharaoh's daughter came down to the river to bathe, as she did at the same time every day. "What is that in the reeds?" she asked. "It looks like a basket."

One of her servants brought the basket to her. "It's a baby!" exclaimed the princess. "It must be one of the Israelite children. I shall save him and he shall be my son."

All this time, Miriam had been hiding in the reeds, watching out for her baby brother. "Your Highness," she said. "I know an Israelite woman who will nurse the baby for you."

"Good," said the princess. "The baby must have milk."

So the baby was taken care of by his own mother until he was old enough to go to the palace and live with Pharaoh's family.

The princess called the baby Moses, which means "taken from the water."

Many years later, God chose Moses to lead the Israelites to freedom.

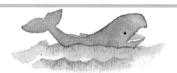

Jonah and the Big Fish

The Israelites became a great nation, but as God watched over His Earth, He saw that the people of Nineveh were very wicked and violent. He asked an Israelite teacher named Jonah to go and talk to them.

But Jonah didn't like that idea at all. He didn't want to go to Nineveh.

He ran away from God and boarded a ship that was going to Tarshish, in the other direction.

God knew that Jonah was on the ship and He sent a great storm. All the sailors were terrified.

When Jonah realized what was happening, he told the sailors that the storm was his fault. "I tried to disobey God," he said. "You had better throw me over the side."

The sailors didn't want to do it, but Jonah made them throw him into the water. Immediately, the wind dropped and the sea became calm.

37

Jonah fell through the waves, sure that he was going to drown. All of a sudden, a huge fish came up and opened its jaws. Down . . .

and down and down

the dark . . .

through the water into

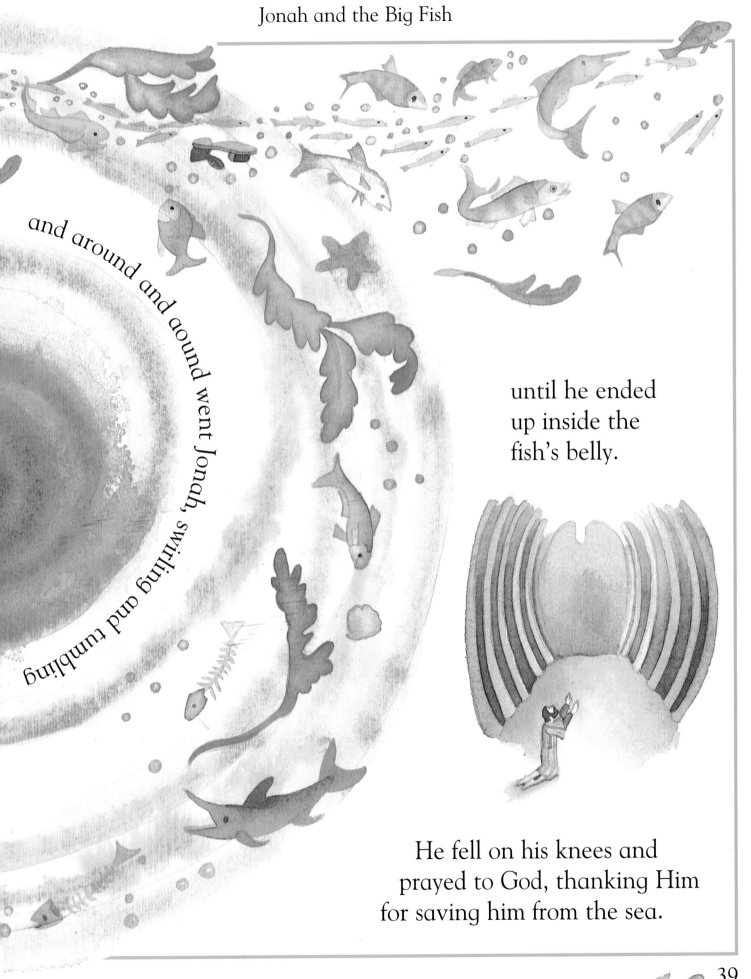

and around and around went Jonah, swirling and tumbling

until he ended up inside the fish's belly.

He fell on his knees and prayed to God, thanking Him for saving him from the sea.

After three days and nights, God thought Jonah had learned his lesson. He made the fish swim to the shore . . .

and there it threw Jonah up onto the land. "Well?" asked God. "Now will you go to Nineveh?"

So Jonah walked all the way to Nineveh.

He warned all the people that God would destroy the city if they didn't stop doing bad things.

Everyone, even the king, was sorry. They all promised to lead better lives in the future. So God did not have to destroy the people after all. He was glad He could forgive them.

Daniel in the Lions' Den

Many Israelites strayed from God, till in time He let the Jewish homeland be conquered and its people carried off into exile. One Jew who still trusted God was Daniel.

Daniel was so honest and wise that the king, Darius, made him prime minister. All the other politicians were jealous.

They made Darius pass a law saying no one should pray to anyone but the king. Anyone who did would be thrown into a pit with hungry lions.

But Daniel went on praying to God the way he always had. Everyone could see him.

"Daniel prays to God," said the jealous politicians to Darius. "He has broken your law. You must throw him to the lions."

Darius was sad. He liked Daniel, but the law was the law.

He ordered Daniel to be thrown into the lions' den.

Next morning, the king went sadly to the lions' den, not daring to hope that Daniel had been saved.

"Daniel! Has your God kept you safe from the lions?"

"Here I am. God's angel stood between me and the lions."

The king ordered that Daniel be taken out of the pit. He had the politicians thrown in instead and the lions made short work of them, munching on their bones.

Then Darius ordered all his people to respect Daniel's God.

Who's Who in the Bible Stories

To help you find your way around **A First Book of Jewish Bible Stories**, here is a list of main characters and the pages where you'll find them. There's also a reference showing where the stories are in the Bible.

Noah   Page 12

Genesis 6–9

The only good man of his time. God sent a big flood to wash the world clean of wickedness. Only Noah, his family, and two of each animal were saved.

Adam and Eve   Page 7

Genesis 1–3

The first man and woman.

Shem, Ham,   Page 12
and Japheth

Genesis 6–9

Noah's three sons.

Abraham Page 20

Genesis 12–13, 17, 21–22

A descendant of Noah who had great faith in God. We remember him as the first Jew.

Sarah Page 20

Genesis 12–13, 17, 21–22

Abraham's wife. God gave her a son when she was past child-bearing age.

Isaac Page 22

Genesis 21–22

Son of Abraham and Sarah.

Lot Page 21

Genesis 13

Abraham's nephew.

Rebekah Page 24

Genesis 25

Isaac's wife. They had twin sons, Esau and Jacob.

Jacob Page 24

Genesis 37, 42–45

Also known as Israel, the younger son of Isaac and Rebekah. He had two wives, Leah and Rachel, and twelve sons, Reuben, Simeon, Levi, Judah, Issachar, Zebulun, Gad, Asher, Dan, Naphtali, Joseph, and Benjamin.

Joseph and Benjamin Page 24

Genesis 37, 39–45

Jacob's two youngest sons. Their mother was Rachel, the woman Jacob loved the most. Joseph always looked after his little brother Benjamin, even when they were grown up.

Pharaoh Page 28, 32

Genesis 40–41, Exodus 1

The title given to kings of Egypt.

Israelites Page 32

Exodus 1

Descendants of Jacob and his family.

Miriam Page 32

Exodus 2

Moses' older sister.

Moses Page 32

Exodus 2

An Israelite. Brought up as an Egyptian. God chose him to lead the Israelites to freedom.

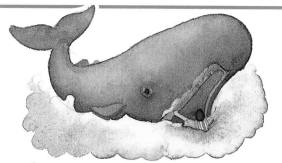

Jonah Page 36

Jonah 1–4

An Israelite preacher and a reluctant hero. When God asked him to go to Nineveh, he refused. An adventure with a large fish changed his mind.

Darius Page 42

Daniel 6

A Persian king who made Daniel his prime minister but was tricked into sending Daniel into the lions' den.

Daniel Page 42

Daniel 6

A Jewish exile in Babylon, whose faith in God was put to the test.